Tangled in the Light

poems by

Elizabeth Threadgill

Finishing Line Press
Georgetown, Kentucky

Tangled in the Light

Copyright © 2018 by Elizabeth Threadgill
ISBN 978-1-63534-470-7 First Edition
All rights reserved under International and Pan-American Copyright Conventions.
No part of this book may be reproduced in any manner whatsoever without written
permission from the publisher, except in the case of brief quotations embodied in
critical articles and reviews.

ACKNOWLEDGMENTS

Much appreciation to Kathleen Peirce, Roger Jones, Cyrus Cassells, Trey Moody, and James Henry Knippen.

Publisher: Leah Maines
Editor: Christen Kincaid
Cover Art: James Henry Knippen
Author Photo: James Henry Knippen

Printed in the USA on acid-free paper.
Order online: www.finishinglinepress.com
         also available on amazon.com

                Author inquiries and mail orders:
                      Finishing Line Press
                        P. O. Box 1626
                 Georgetown, Kentucky 40324
                           U. S. A.

Table of Contents

Doe 1

Rifle Fire 2

Rabbit 3

Reverberation 4

Morning 5

Crickets 6

Hay Flecks 7

Apples 8

Goat 9

Duck 10

Snails 11

Duck Feathers 12

Immensity 13

Fields 14

Rabbits 15

Faraway 16

Fireflies 17

Stars Splitting 18

Moth 19

Cracked Light 20

Stars 21

Life 22

for James

In truth each day is a universe in which
we are tangled in the light of stars.

—Jim Harrison

Doe

a doe stops on the edge of reason
just outside the glow
just outside my self
I keep her in my periphery
like a silk scarf
tucked in a jacket sleeve
brushing the back of my hand
knowing it could fall away at any moment

Rifle Fire

dove rifled like a drawer
turned out, sun falling
behind a shelf—the sound of it
deafening like a shelf
turned out, sun falling
out, over the world, fire blazing
wings failing, burning, down

Rabbit

to have flinched at the rabbit—
heart fluttering faster than mine—
but wouldn't doves
have taught better the blind, wild fear
hurdling out of tall grass
whirring past my ear like shrapnel
cutting the air with singular purpose

Reverberation

ringing tied to steel
like a dog
too many circles
around a post
so too
we are never undone

Morning

haze off the hides of cows
like a dressing screen
for the day
egrets nearby
with their paper eyes
everything waking

Crickets

soothsayers of the coming
of birds and their trinkets

shining hay grasses to weave
among the roof's scantling

Hay Flecks

at the back of the throat
a hawk's talons
pin a little pink rabbit

Apples

opening apples for the ass
a breath of mandala
at the core
palm outstretched—
she is a steward
of this and next

Goat
> *For Eve*

the goat is singing
half-songs rolled
in sweet grain
joyous tongue
like the child making
moons with her mouth

Duck

from below
with her long feet
skating across the glass
of this world
into the next
with more ease
and grace than we
are allotted

Snails

stony trove
along a river bank
eaten clean
by birds and raccoons
leaving little
Eskimo coats

Duck Feathers

because they are like radiant bone
splintering outward

her dress pouring from her
as she wades into the after

Immensity

clouds are only a forest
pinefeathers
stretching between skylines

but stars exhaust
what we are

Fields

fields laid over
by wind

a bed of flat-grass
to tease cow mouths

deer hollows
gathered and pressed

a sheet of golden sparrows
sunning wing-to-wing

Rabbits

on the horizon
silhouettes akin
to wings and knives

blood-pink
like plum skin
against time

Faraway

in the deep deep shining
before the hour
a smoldering quilt
laid out over dried fields
of mice and rabbits

Fireflies

sundancers at dusk
fire-tipped Morse
code flickering in the air
fractured but buoyant
in the net of space

Stars Splitting

stars splitting
slipping past
our consciousness
like acorn shells
tossed by squirrels
with no sense of urgency

Moth

a moth caught in the tendrils
behind your ear
wings dancing there
wilted petals in a breeze

to pluck it
like a dusty coin
monuments fly free
back into space
swinging far

Cracked Light

stars open
like eggs broken
over cast iron
firing shards
of shells
overhead

Stars

we sit, faces upturned
like the cat counting moth wings
covered with the dust of them all

Life

comes before
the stars break
showering
our heads
with sparks
as if we are
the welders
as if we
are engineers
of our arcs
as if
we were
the architects
of sight

Elizabeth Threadgill grew up in Marfa, Texas, a community rich in art, poetry, and rabbits. Later, with her husband, poet James Henry Knippen, she resided in a small blue house adjacent to a field of cows in Martindale, Texas. *Tangled in the Light* marks Elizabeth's poetry debut and is representative of landscape and life in rural Texas. She holds an MFA in Poetry and a PhD in Developmental Education-Literacy, both from Texas State University. She recently moved to upstate New York, where she is an Assistant Professor of English at Utica College.

www.ingramcontent.com/pod-product-compliance
Lightning Source LLC
LaVergne TN
LVHW041520070426
835507LV00012B/1705